Satellite Solutions Harnessing

Business Potential in the Space Industry

Ahmed

Satellite Solutions Harnessing Business Potential in the Space Industry
Copyright © 2023 by Ahmed

The first edition was published in 2023

ISBN:

Published by:
Sunshine
1663 Liberty Drive
Hyderabad, IN 47403
www.Sunshinepublishers.com

This book is self-published using on-demand printing and publishing, which allows it to be printed and distributed globally

TABLE OF CONTENT

Chapter 8: Scaling and Expanding a Satellite Company 00

Chapter 9: Future Outlook and Trends in the Space Industry 00

Chapter 10: Conclusion 00

Chapter 1: Introduction to the Space Industry

Overview of the space industry

The space industry has witnessed tremendous growth and innovation in recent years, presenting an array of exciting opportunities for entrepreneurs looking to venture into this niche. This subchapter will provide an overview of the space industry, highlighting its potential and the various sectors within it.

The space industry encompasses a wide range of activities related to the exploration, utilization, and commercialization of space. It is no longer limited to government agencies and scientific research but has expanded to include private companies and startups seeking to capitalize on the immense potential offered by space technology.

One of the key drivers of the space industry is satellite technology. Satellites play a crucial role in communication, navigation, weather forecasting, and Earth observation. Entrepreneurs in the space industry can leverage satellite solutions to provide innovative services such as satellite internet connectivity, remote sensing, and data analytics. These applications have the potential to transform various sectors, including agriculture, logistics, telecommunications, and disaster management.

Another exciting aspect of the space industry is space tourism. With the rise of companies like SpaceX and Blue Origin, space travel is no longer confined to astronauts. Entrepreneurs can now explore opportunities in the emerging space tourism sector by offering unique experiences and packages for individuals who dream of venturing beyond Earth's atmosphere.

Furthermore, space mining is an area within the space industry that holds immense potential. The mining of asteroids and the moon for valuable resources such as rare metals and water could revolutionize industries on Earth, including manufacturing and energy production. Entrepreneurs can explore partnerships and technologies to tap into this nascent yet promising field.

Collaboration and partnerships are essential in the space industry. Entrepreneurs can collaborate with government agencies, established space companies, and research institutions to access resources, knowledge, and funding. The space industry thrives on innovation and requires a multidisciplinary approach, making it an exciting field for entrepreneurs with diverse backgrounds.

However, it is important to note that the space industry also comes with its own set of challenges. The high costs, technical complexities, and regulatory frameworks can be daunting. Entrepreneurs must be prepared to invest in research and development, navigate legal and regulatory requirements, and manage risks associated with space missions.

In conclusion, the space industry offers immense business potential for entrepreneurs. With advancements in satellite technology, space tourism, and space mining, this industry is undergoing a transformation that presents numerous opportunities. Entrepreneurs can harness the power of space to develop innovative solutions and contribute to the growth of various sectors. However, it is crucial to stay informed, collaborate with industry stakeholders, and navigate the challenges associated with venturing into this exciting and dynamic field.

Growth and potential of the space industry

The space industry, once limited to government agencies and scientific exploration, has now become a thriving sector with immense business potential. Entrepreneurs interested in the space niche have a unique opportunity to tap into a market that is expanding at an unprecedented rate. In this subchapter, we will explore the growth and potential of the space industry, highlighting the various opportunities that await entrepreneurs in this exciting field.

Over the past decade, the space industry has witnessed a significant transformation driven by advancements in technology, reduced costs, and increased private sector involvement. Today, private companies are launching satellites, providing communication services, and even planning manned missions to outer space. This rapid growth is fueled by the increasing demand for satellite-based applications, such as global internet connectivity, Earth observation, and navigation systems.

One of the most promising areas within the space industry is satellite communications. With the advent of new satellite constellations, entrepreneurs can now offer affordable and high-speed internet connectivity to underserved regions around the world. This presents an opportunity for entrepreneurs to develop innovative business models that cater to the growing demand for connectivity in remote areas.

Another area with tremendous potential is Earth observation. Satellites equipped with advanced imaging sensors can capture valuable data about our planet, enabling entrepreneurs to provide insights and solutions in various sectors, such as agriculture, environmental monitoring, and urban planning. By leveraging this data, entrepreneurs can create products and services that help industries optimize their operations and make informed decisions.

Furthermore, the space industry offers opportunities for entrepreneurs interested in space tourism and exploration. With the rise of private space companies, the dream of space travel is becoming a reality. Entrepreneurs can capitalize on this trend by developing technologies, services, and experiences that cater to the growing demand for space tourism. This includes designing spacecraft, organizing spaceflights, and creating immersive experiences for individuals to explore the wonders of space.

As the space industry continues to grow, entrepreneurs need to stay abreast of the latest technological advancements and market trends. Collaboration with other players in the industry, both within and outside the space niche, can also be beneficial. By fostering partnerships and leveraging collective expertise, entrepreneurs can unlock the full potential of the space industry and drive innovation.

In conclusion, the space industry is experiencing unprecedented growth, presenting ample opportunities for entrepreneurs to harness its business potential. Whether through satellite communications, Earth observation, or space tourism, entrepreneurs can carve out a niche in this exciting field and develop innovative solutions that address the evolving needs of our planet and beyond. By staying ahead of the curve and embracing collaboration, entrepreneurs can thrive in the dynamic and promising space industry.

Importance of satellite solutions in the space industry

The Importance of Satellite Solutions in the Space Industry

In the vast realm of the space industry, satellite solutions have emerged as the backbone of various entrepreneurial ventures. Entrepreneurs seeking to harness the business potential of space must understand the profound importance of satellite solutions and how they have revolutionized the industry.

Satellite solutions play a pivotal role in enabling communication, navigation, and Earth observation, among other essential functions. They have transformed the way we communicate globally, bridging distances and connecting people like never before. Satellites allow entrepreneurs to establish seamless communication networks in remote areas, enabling businesses to expand their reach and tap into new markets. Furthermore, they have facilitated the development of advanced navigation systems, enhancing logistics and transportation, ultimately leading to more efficient supply chains and improved customer service.

The space industry has also witnessed a surge in the demand for Earth observation data. Satellites provide entrepreneurs with invaluable insights into various aspects of our planet, such as climate patterns, natural resource management, and urban planning. This data empowers entrepreneurs to make informed decisions, optimize operations, and develop sustainable business practices. For instance, agricultural entrepreneurs can leverage satellite imagery to monitor crop health, detect potential issues, and optimize irrigation and fertilization practices. Similarly, urban planners can utilize satellite data to design smarter cities, reduce energy consumption, and enhance the overall quality of life.

Moreover, satellite solutions have revolutionized scientific research and exploration. They have enabled entrepreneurs to conduct experiments and collect data in outer space, advancing our understanding of the universe and opening up new possibilities for technological innovation. From studying distant celestial bodies to monitoring space weather, satellites have played a pivotal role in expanding our knowledge and pushing the boundaries of human exploration.

In the competitive realm of the space industry, entrepreneurs must recognize the significance of satellite solutions. They have become the lifeline for various entrepreneurial ventures, offering unparalleled opportunities for growth and innovation. However, it is crucial for entrepreneurs to stay abreast of the latest advancements in satellite technology and carefully evaluate the various solutions available. This will help them make informed decisions and leverage satellite capabilities to their fullest potential.

In conclusion, the importance of satellite solutions in the space industry cannot be overstated. They have transformed the way we communicate, navigate, and observe our planet and beyond. For entrepreneurs in the space industry, understanding the role and significance of satellite solutions is paramount to harnessing the immense business potential that this industry has to offer. By leveraging the power of satellite solutions, entrepreneurs can unlock new horizons and drive innovation in the ever-evolving space industry.

Objectives of the book

Welcome to "Satellite Solutions: Harnessing Business Potential in the Space Industry," a comprehensive guidebook specifically designed for entrepreneurs in the niche of space. This subchapter will delve into the key objectives of this book, providing you with a sneak peek into the valuable knowledge and insights you can expect to gain from its pages.

1. Understanding the Space Industry: The primary objective of this book is to provide entrepreneurs with a deep understanding of the space industry. It will explore the history, current trends, and future prospects of the space sector, giving you a solid foundation to navigate this dynamic and ever-evolving industry.

2. Identifying Business Opportunities: By examining the space industry's various segments and their interdependencies, this book aims to help entrepreneurs identify lucrative business opportunities. Whether you are interested in satellite manufacturing, launch services, satellite data analysis, or any other space-related venture, this book will equip you with the necessary knowledge to make informed decisions.

3. Assessing Risks and Challenges: Every business venture comes with its own set of risks and challenges. In this book, we will delve into the potential risks and challenges associated with space entrepreneurship. By understanding these obstacles in advance, you can develop effective strategies to mitigate risks and overcome challenges, ensuring the success of your business.

4. Developing Effective Business Models: This book aims to guide entrepreneurs in developing effective business models tailored to the space industry. From revenue generation strategies to cost optimization techniques, you

will learn how to create a sustainable and profitable business model that aligns with the unique characteristics of the space sector.

5. Networking and Collaborations: The space industry thrives on collaboration and partnerships. This book will emphasize the importance of networking and provide practical tips on building relationships within the space community. You will learn how to leverage partnerships to enhance your business prospects and gain a competitive edge in the market.

6. Regulatory and Legal Framework: The space industry is subject to complex regulatory and legal frameworks. Understanding these regulations is crucial for entrepreneurs to ensure compliance and avoid potential legal pitfalls. In this book, we will examine the key legal aspects of the space industry, enabling you to navigate this intricate landscape with confidence.

"Satellite Solutions: Harnessing Business Potential in the Space Industry" is your ultimate guide to unlocking the immense business potential that the space industry offers. Whether you are a seasoned entrepreneur looking to venture into the space sector or a budding entrepreneur with a passion for space, this book will equip you with the knowledge, insights, and tools necessary for success. Get ready to launch your space business to new heights!

Chapter 2: Understanding Space Entrepreneurship

Definition and scope of space entrepreneurship

Space entrepreneurship refers to the process of identifying, creating, and pursuing business opportunities within the space industry. It encompasses the development and utilization of space technologies, services, and products for commercial purposes. In recent years, the space sector has witnessed a significant transformation, moving away from a primarily government-led domain to a more dynamic and commercially driven industry. This has opened up numerous opportunities for entrepreneurs to enter the space market and contribute to its growth and innovation.

The scope of space entrepreneurship is vast, covering various sectors and industries within the space ecosystem. Entrepreneurs in this field can engage in activities such as satellite communication, Earth observation, space tourism, launch services, space mining, and space manufacturing, among others. The potential applications of space technology are diverse, ranging from telecommunications and broadcasting to weather forecasting, navigation, and environmental monitoring.

One of the key drivers behind the rise of space entrepreneurship is the increasing accessibility and affordability of space technologies. Advancements in miniaturization, reusable rocket technology, and cost reductions in satellite manufacturing have democratized access to space, allowing startups and small businesses to enter the industry. This has led to a surge in innovation and the emergence of new business models, disrupting traditional players and creating new market opportunities.

Space entrepreneurs face unique challenges that set this industry apart from others. The inherent complexities of space technology, regulatory frameworks, and high capital requirements make it a high-risk, high-reward sector. However, with the right expertise, innovative thinking, and strategic partnerships, entrepreneurs can overcome these challenges and capitalize on the immense potential of the space industry.

To succeed in space entrepreneurship, entrepreneurs must possess a combination of technical knowledge, business acumen, and a deep understanding of the evolving market dynamics. They need to stay updated with the latest developments in space technology, regulatory changes, and market trends. Collaboration and partnerships with established space companies, government agencies, and research institutions can also be instrumental in gaining access to resources, expertise, and funding.

In conclusion, space entrepreneurship offers a unique and exciting opportunity for entrepreneurs to enter the space industry and contribute to its growth and development. The scope of space entrepreneurship is vast, covering various sectors within the space ecosystem. With advancements in technology and a more commercially driven approach, the space industry is ripe with potential for innovative business models and disruptive solutions. By staying informed, fostering partnerships, and leveraging their expertise, entrepreneurs can navigate the challenges and harness the business potential of the space industry.

Evolution of space entrepreneurship

In the ever-expanding realm of space exploration and satellite technology, the rise of space entrepreneurship has been nothing short of remarkable. This subchapter delves into the fascinating journey of how space entrepreneurship has evolved over time, highlighting the significant milestones and key players that have shaped the industry into what it is today. For entrepreneurs with an interest in the space niche, understanding this evolution is crucial to harnessing the immense business potential present in the space industry.

The roots of space entrepreneurship can be traced back to the mid-20th century, when governments and national space agencies were the sole players in space exploration. However, with the advent of the private sector's participation, the dynamics of the space industry underwent a dramatic shift. The turning point came with the launch of the first privately funded satellite, Intelsat I, in 1965. This feat demonstrated the viability of commercial space ventures and set the stage for future entrepreneurs to enter the market.

In the following decades, several visionary entrepreneurs emerged, each making their mark on the space industry. Companies like SpaceX, Blue Origin, and Virgin Galactic have become synonymous with space entrepreneurship, revolutionizing the sector with their innovative technologies and business models. SpaceX, founded by Elon Musk, has pioneered reusable rockets and drastically reduced the cost of space launches. Blue Origin, led by Jeff Bezos, has focused on developing reusable spacecraft and creating a sustainable infrastructure for space travel. Virgin Galactic, led by Richard Branson, aims to make suborbital space tourism a reality for the general public.

The evolution of space entrepreneurship has not been limited to launch services alone. The development of satellite technologies and applications has opened up new avenues for entrepreneurs to explore. From Earth observation and weather forecasting to telecommunication and navigation, satellites have become indispensable tools for various industries. Startups like Planet Labs and OneWeb have leveraged advancements in miniaturization and constellation-based networks to provide affordable, high-resolution satellite imagery and global broadband connectivity.

Furthermore, the emergence of new funding models, such as venture capital and crowdfunding platforms, has democratized access to capital for space entrepreneurs. This has allowed small startups and innovators to compete in an industry that was once dominated by well-funded government agencies and large corporations. The rise of space-focused incubators and accelerators has also provided crucial support and mentorship to budding entrepreneurs, nurturing a vibrant ecosystem of space startups.

As space exploration continues to capture the public's imagination and governments strive to establish a sustainable presence beyond Earth, the opportunities for entrepreneurs in the space industry are boundless. By understanding the evolution of space entrepreneurship and staying abreast of the latest trends and technologies, entrepreneurs can position themselves at the forefront of this dynamic field and unlock its vast business potential. Whether it's launching satellites, developing satellite applications, or investing in space startups, the future of space entrepreneurship holds immense promise for those willing to venture into the final frontier.

Challenges and opportunities in space entrepreneurship

Introduction:
Space exploration and technology have opened up a new era of possibilities for entrepreneurs. The space industry offers a vast array of opportunities for those willing to challenge the limits of innovation. However, with these opportunities come unique challenges that entrepreneurs must navigate to succeed in the space sector. This subchapter explores the challenges and opportunities faced by entrepreneurs in the space industry, providing valuable insights for those seeking to harness the business potential of space.

Challenges:

1. Technological hurdles: Developing space-related technologies requires significant investments in research and development. Entrepreneurs must overcome various technical challenges, such as designing efficient satellite systems, creating advanced propulsion systems, and ensuring reliable communication networks.

2. Regulatory constraints: The space industry is subject to stringent regulations imposed by governments and international bodies. Entrepreneurs must comply with licensing requirements, spectrum allocation, and safety regulations, which can be time-consuming and costly.

3. Financial barriers: Space projects demand substantial financial resources due to the high costs associated with research, manufacturing, and launch. Entrepreneurs must secure funding from private investors, government grants, or partnerships to sustain their ventures.

4. Infrastructure limitations: Despite recent advancements, space infrastructure remains limited. Entrepreneurs face the challenge of building or accessing launch facilities, ground stations, and satellite networks to support their operations.

Opportunities:

1. Satellite communications: Entrepreneurs can capitalize on the increasing demand for satellite-based communication services, such as broadband internet, remote sensing, and global navigation systems. These services have enormous potential in areas lacking terrestrial connectivity.

2. Earth observation and data analytics: Satellites provide valuable data for monitoring climate change, natural disasters, and urban development. Entrepreneurs can leverage this information to develop innovative applications in sectors like agriculture, logistics, and urban planning.

3. Space tourism and exploration: The emerging space tourism industry offers exciting opportunities for entrepreneurs. Companies can develop space tourism experiences, suborbital flights, or lunar expeditions for individuals seeking extraordinary adventures.

4. Collaborations and partnerships: Entrepreneurs can maximize their chances of success by forming strategic alliances with established players in the space industry. Collaborations can provide access to infrastructure, expertise, and funding, reducing barriers to entry.

Conclusion:
The challenges in space entrepreneurship should not deter ambitious entrepreneurs from venturing into this exciting industry. By embracing the opportunities presented by satellite communications, earth observation, space tourism, and collaborations, entrepreneurs can harness the business potential of the space industry. Success in the space sector requires a combination of technological innovation, regulatory compliance, financial acumen, and strategic partnerships. With determination, vision, and a willingness to push the boundaries of human achievement, entrepreneurs can contribute to the continued growth and exploration of space.

Key skills and traits for space entrepreneurs

In the rapidly evolving space industry, entrepreneurship has become an essential avenue for driving innovation and creating new business opportunities. To succeed in this unique and challenging sector, aspiring space entrepreneurs must possess a specific set of skills and traits that will enable them to navigate the complexities of the space industry. This subchapter explores the key skills and traits that are crucial for individuals looking to venture into the realm of space entrepreneurship.

1. Technical expertise: Space entrepreneurship requires a solid understanding of various technical aspects, including satellite technology, rocket science, and space systems. Entrepreneurs should possess a strong foundation in engineering, physics, and other relevant disciplines to effectively develop and manage space-related ventures.

2. Adaptability and resilience: The space industry is characterized by its fast-paced nature and constant technological advancements. Therefore, entrepreneurs must be adaptable to changing circumstances and be resilient in the face of setbacks or failures. Flexibility and the ability to learn from mistakes are key traits for success in this industry.

3. Visionary mindset: Space entrepreneurs need to possess a visionary mindset and the ability to think outside the box. They must be able to identify potential market opportunities and develop innovative solutions that can address the evolving needs of the space industry. A forward-thinking approach is essential for staying ahead of the competition.

4. Business acumen: While technical knowledge is crucial, space entrepreneurs must also possess strong business acumen. This includes skills in strategic planning, financial

management, marketing, and negotiation. Understanding market dynamics and having the ability to identify profitable business models are vital for sustainable growth in the space industry.

5. Collaboration and networking: The space industry is highly collaborative, with numerous stakeholders including government agencies, space organizations, and private companies. Effective collaboration and networking skills are essential for establishing partnerships, securing funding, and accessing necessary resources. Building a strong professional network can also provide valuable mentorship and support.

6. Passion and perseverance: Space entrepreneurship is not for the faint-hearted. The journey can be long and challenging, requiring immense passion and perseverance. Entrepreneurs must be driven by a deep love for space exploration and a strong desire to make a positive impact in the industry.

In conclusion, space entrepreneurship presents unique opportunities and challenges that require a specific skill set and mindset. By cultivating technical expertise, adaptability, visionary thinking, business acumen, collaboration, and a strong passion for space, entrepreneurs can position themselves for success in this exciting and promising industry.

Chapter 3: Identifying Business Opportunities in the Space Industry

Market analysis of the space industry

The space industry has witnessed remarkable growth and transformation over the past few decades. With advancements in technology and an increasing interest in space exploration, the market for space-related products and services has expanded significantly. This subchapter aims to provide entrepreneurs in the space niche with a comprehensive market analysis of the space industry, highlighting key trends, opportunities, and challenges.

The space industry encompasses a wide range of sectors, including satellite manufacturing, launch services, satellite communication, Earth observation, and space tourism, among others. Each sector presents unique opportunities for entrepreneurs to tap into, but it is crucial to understand the market dynamics and trends to make informed business decisions.

One key trend in the space industry is the growing demand for satellite communication. With the ever-increasing need for global connectivity, satellite-based communication services have become indispensable. Entrepreneurs can explore opportunities in providing satellite internet services, mobile satellite communication, and satellite broadcasting.

Another significant trend is the rise of Earth observation and remote sensing technologies. Satellites equipped with high-resolution cameras and sensors are being deployed to gather valuable data for various applications such as agriculture, urban planning, and disaster management. Entrepreneurs can develop innovative solutions by leveraging this data to offer services like precision agriculture, urban analytics, and environmental monitoring.

Furthermore, the space tourism sector is gaining traction, with companies like SpaceX and Blue Origin pioneering commercial space travel. Entrepreneurs can explore opportunities in this niche by offering space tourism experiences, developing technologies to enhance the safety and comfort of space travel, or even building infrastructure for spaceports.

While the space industry offers immense potential, it also poses several challenges. One major challenge is the high cost associated with satellite manufacturing and launching. Entrepreneurs need to carefully consider the financial implications and seek partnerships or funding opportunities to mitigate these costs.

Additionally, the regulatory environment surrounding the space industry is complex and constantly evolving. Entrepreneurs must navigate through various legal and regulatory frameworks to ensure compliance and avoid potential barriers to market entry.

In conclusion, the space industry presents a plethora of opportunities for entrepreneurs looking to harness its business potential. Understanding the market dynamics, trends, and challenges is crucial for making informed business decisions. By capitalizing on the growing demand for satellite communication, Earth observation, and space tourism, entrepreneurs can establish themselves as key players in the space industry, contributing to its continued growth and innovation.

Emerging trends in the space industry

The space industry has always been a captivating field, with its exploration of the unknown and its potential for groundbreaking innovation. In recent years, however, the industry has experienced a surge in emerging trends that are revolutionizing the way we think about space and its business potential. This subchapter explores some of the most significant trends in the space industry today, with a particular focus on their implications for entrepreneurs and the niches of space.

One of the most prominent trends in the space industry is the rise of small satellites, also known as CubeSats. These miniature satellites, often no larger than a shoebox, have opened up new avenues for entrepreneurs to enter the space market. They are significantly cheaper to build and launch compared to traditional satellites, making them accessible to startups and small businesses. This trend has led to an influx of innovative ideas and applications, ranging from Earth observation and telecommunications to weather monitoring and scientific research. Entrepreneurs in the space industry can leverage the growing demand for small satellite services and develop niche solutions to cater to specific customer needs.

Another emerging trend is the commercialization of space exploration. Previously dominated by government agencies, space exploration is now being driven by private companies such as SpaceX and Blue Origin. These companies are not only focused on launching satellites but also on developing reusable rockets and ultimately enabling human colonization of other planets. This trend presents a myriad of opportunities for entrepreneurs, from manufacturing components for space missions to providing support services for space tourists. Entrepreneurs with a passion for space can tap into this growing market and contribute to the advancement of space exploration.

Space tourism is yet another trend that holds immense potential for entrepreneurs. With companies like Virgin Galactic and SpaceX aiming to make space travel accessible to the public, the space tourism industry is on the verge of becoming a reality. Entrepreneurs can seize this opportunity by creating unique experiences for space tourists, such as zero-gravity hotels or lunar excursions. Additionally, the rise of space tourism will require the development of supporting infrastructure, such as spaceports and launch facilities, creating numerous business opportunities in this niche.

In conclusion, the space industry is experiencing a wave of emerging trends that present exciting possibilities for entrepreneurs. The rise of small satellites, the commercialization of space exploration, and the advent of space tourism are just a few examples of the transformative changes taking place in this field. Entrepreneurs with a passion for space can leverage these trends to develop innovative solutions, tap into niche markets, and contribute to the growth and development of the space industry.

Potential business ideas in satellite solutions

As the space industry continues to evolve and expand, opportunities for entrepreneurs within the field of satellite solutions are multiplying. The integration of space technology into everyday life has created a wide range of potential business ideas that can capitalize on the growing demand for satellite solutions. In this subchapter, we will explore some of the most promising business ideas in this niche, aimed specifically at entrepreneurs in the space industry.

1. Satellite Internet Service Providers (ISPs): With the increasing need for high-speed internet connectivity in remote areas, there is a significant potential for entrepreneurs to establish satellite ISPs. By leveraging satellite technology, entrepreneurs can provide internet access to underserved regions, enabling connectivity and bridging the digital divide.

2. Earth Observation Services: Satellites equipped with advanced imaging sensors can capture high-resolution images and data about our planet. Entrepreneurs can leverage this technology to provide earth observation services, catering to various industries such as agriculture, urban planning, environmental monitoring, and disaster management.

3. Fleet Tracking and Management: Satellites can be used to track and manage fleets of vehicles or vessels, providing real-time monitoring, route optimization, and maintenance updates. Entrepreneurs can develop innovative solutions that leverage satellite data to enhance fleet management operations, increasing efficiency and reducing costs.

4. Remote Sensing for Resource Exploration: Satellites equipped with remote sensing capabilities can provide valuable insights into natural resource exploration.

Entrepreneurs have the potential to offer satellite-based solutions for mining, oil and gas exploration, and other resource-intensive industries, enabling more accurate and efficient exploration processes.

5. Satellite Communication Solutions: Satellites play a crucial role in global communication. Entrepreneurs can develop innovative communication solutions, such as satellite phones or messaging systems, aiming to provide reliable connectivity in areas with limited or no terrestrial infrastructure.

6. Weather Forecasting and Climate Monitoring: Satellites equipped with weather and climate sensors can provide real-time data for accurate weather forecasting and climate monitoring. Entrepreneurs can capitalize on this technology by offering specialized weather services, targeting industries like agriculture, aviation, and disaster preparedness.

7. Space Tourism Services: With the rise of commercial space travel, entrepreneurs can explore opportunities in the space tourism sector. This can include designing and operating satellites that offer unique and immersive experiences for tourists, as well as providing support services for space tourism companies.

These are just a few of the potential business ideas in satellite solutions that entrepreneurs can pursue in the space industry. With the advancements in satellite technology, the possibilities are vast and ever-expanding. By harnessing the power of satellites, entrepreneurs have the opportunity to create innovative solutions that not only address current challenges but also shape the future of various industries. With the right vision, expertise, and determination, entrepreneurs can carve a niche for themselves in the exciting world of satellite solutions.

Evaluating the feasibility of space business ideas

Introduction:
As entrepreneurs in the space industry, it is crucial to thoroughly evaluate the feasibility of your business ideas before diving into the vast opportunities that outer space offers. This subchapter aims to provide you with key insights on how to assess the feasibility of your space business ideas, ensuring you make informed decisions that maximize your potential for success.

Market   Research:
Before embarking on any space business venture, conducting comprehensive market research is essential. Identify potential customers, competitors, and market trends within the space industry. Space exploration, satellite communication, Earth observation, and space tourism are just a few areas worth exploring. Understanding the demands and gaps in the market will allow you to tailor your business idea accordingly.

Technical   Feasibility:
Evaluate the technical feasibility of your space business idea by considering aspects such as the required technology, infrastructure, and expertise. Collaborate with experts and engineers to assess the viability of your concept and identify potential challenges. This evaluation will help you determine if your idea can be realistically implemented within the current technological landscape.

Financial   Viability:
Analyzing the financial feasibility of your space business idea is crucial for long-term success. Consider the costs associated with research and development, production, marketing, and distribution. Evaluate potential revenue streams, such as product sales, services, or partnerships, and estimate the return on investment. It is important to

have a clear understanding of the financial implications and potential profitability of your venture.

Legal and Regulatory Compliance: Navigating the legal and regulatory landscape of the space industry is essential. Familiarize yourself with international and national laws, licensing requirements, and intellectual property rights. Ensure that your business idea aligns with the legal frameworks and obtain any necessary permits or licenses. Compliance with regulations will mitigate risks and provide a solid foundation for your business.

Risk Assessment: Conduct a comprehensive risk assessment to identify potential threats to your space business idea. Assess technological risks, market volatility, competition, political stability, and financial risks. Develop contingency plans to mitigate these risks and ensure the resilience of your business.

Conclusion:
Evaluating the feasibility of your space business ideas is critical to ensure their successful implementation and long-term sustainability. By conducting thorough market research, assessing technical and financial viability, complying with legal regulations, and mitigating risks, you can make informed decisions that maximize your chances of success in the dynamic and promising space industry.

Chapter 4: Starting a Satellite Company

Establishing a space startup: Steps and considerations

In the rapidly evolving space industry, entrepreneurs with a passion for exploration and innovation are finding unprecedented opportunities to establish their own space startups. However, venturing into this niche market requires careful planning, strategic decision-making, and an understanding of the unique challenges that come with operating in space. This subchapter is dedicated to guiding aspiring entrepreneurs through the process of establishing a space startup, providing key steps and considerations to ensure a successful launch.

1. Identifying a Niche: Before diving into the space industry, it is essential to identify a specific niche that aligns with your expertise and interests. Research the market to find gaps and opportunities that your startup can fill, whether it's satellite communications, space tourism, or Earth observation.

2. Building a Team: Assembling a team of experts with diverse skill sets is crucial for the success of your space startup. Seek out professionals with a background in aerospace engineering, astrophysics, or business development to ensure a well-rounded and capable team.

3. Developing a Business Plan: A comprehensive business plan is essential for securing funding and attracting potential investors. Outline your startup's mission, target market, revenue streams, and growth strategy. Additionally, consider potential risks and mitigation plans.

4. Securing Funding: Funding a space startup can be a significant challenge due to the high costs associated with research, development, and launch. Explore various

funding options such as government grants, venture capital, crowdfunding, or strategic partnerships to secure the necessary financial support.

5. Regulatory and Legal Considerations: The space industry is heavily regulated to ensure safety and prevent conflicts. Familiarize yourself with international and national laws governing space activities, licensing requirements, liability issues, and export controls.

6. Technology Development: Developing cutting-edge technology is crucial for the success of your space startup. Collaborate with experts to design, build, and test your satellite or spacecraft, ensuring it meets industry standards and objectives.

7. Launch and Operations: Once your technology is ready, carefully plan the launch and operational aspects of your startup. Collaborate with launch service providers, establish ground control stations, and develop protocols for monitoring and maintaining your assets in space.

8. Collaboration and Partnerships: Space startups thrive on collaboration. Seek opportunities to partner with established space companies, universities, research institutions, or government agencies to leverage their expertise, resources, and networks.

9. Marketing and Branding: Establishing a strong brand and marketing strategy is essential for attracting customers and investors. Highlight the unique value proposition of your space startup, communicate your mission, and engage with relevant industry events and conferences.

10. Continuous Innovation: To remain competitive in the rapidly evolving space industry, continuous innovation is vital. Stay updated with emerging technologies, industry trends, and market demands, and invest in research and

development to ensure your startup stays ahead of the curve.

By following these key steps and considering the unique challenges and opportunities in the space industry, entrepreneurs can set themselves on a path towards establishing a successful and impactful space startup. Embrace the spirit of exploration, push the boundaries of technology, and unlock the business potential that lies within the vast expanse of space.

Developing a business plan for a satellite company

In today's rapidly evolving space industry, entrepreneurs have an incredible opportunity to tap into the vast potential of satellite solutions. However, a successful venture in this niche requires careful planning and a well-crafted business plan. This subchapter aims to guide entrepreneurs through the process of developing a comprehensive business plan for a satellite company.

1. Executive Summary: Begin your business plan with a concise summary that highlights the key aspects of your satellite company. Include your mission statement, vision, target market, and unique selling proposition. This section should provide a snapshot of your overall business strategy.

2. Company Description: Describe your satellite company in detail, including its legal structure, ownership, and management team. Highlight the expertise and experience of key personnel involved in the venture. Additionally, explain the specific services or products your company will offer in the space industry.

3. Market Analysis: Conduct a thorough analysis of the space industry and identify potential market segments. Explore the current market trends, competitive landscape, and regulatory environment. Evaluate the demand for satellite solutions and identify your target customers within the space niche.

4. Product or Service Offering: Outline the specific satellite products or services your company will provide. Discuss the unique features, benefits, and advantages of your offerings. Highlight any partnerships or collaborations that enhance your value proposition.

5. Marketing and Sales Strategy: Develop a robust marketing and sales plan to effectively reach your target

audience. Identify the most effective channels to promote your satellite solutions. Establish a pricing strategy that is competitive yet profitable. Detail your sales approach and customer acquisition tactics.

6. Operations and Management: Describe the operational aspects of your satellite company, including the required infrastructure, technology, and human resources. Outline your supply chain management, quality control processes, and any strategic partnerships necessary for successful operations.

7. Financial Projections: Provide a detailed financial forecast that includes revenue projections, operating expenses, and cash flow analysis. Include a break-even analysis and discuss how you plan to fund your satellite company's initial and ongoing operations. Consider potential risks and create contingency plans.

8. Implementation Plan: Lay out a timeline and milestones for executing your business plan. Define the critical tasks and responsibilities required to launch and operate your satellite company successfully. Identify potential obstacles and develop strategies to overcome them.

By following these guidelines, entrepreneurs in the space industry can develop a robust business plan for their satellite company. A well-crafted plan will not only guide the growth and development of the venture but also attract potential investors and partners who recognize the vast business potential in the space industry. Remember, adaptability and continuous improvement are key in this rapidly evolving field, so be prepared to iterate and refine your business plan as needed to stay ahead of the curve.

Funding options for space startups

Introduction:
In the fast-evolving space industry, entrepreneurs looking to venture into the realm of satellite solutions often face the challenge of securing adequate funding to kickstart their projects. This subchapter aims to provide a comprehensive overview of the various funding options available to space startups, equipping entrepreneurs with the knowledge and resources needed to navigate the financial landscape successfully.

1.   Government   Grants   and   Contracts:
One of the primary sources of funding for space startups is government grants and contracts. Many governments across the globe, recognizing the potential of the space industry, offer financial support to entrepreneurs through research and development grants or by awarding contracts for specific projects. Entrepreneurs must actively engage with government agencies and stay updated on funding opportunities to maximize their chances of securing these grants.

2.   Venture   Capital   and   Angel   Investors:
Venture capital firms and angel investors play a crucial role in the space industry by providing early-stage funding to startups with high growth potential. These investors are attracted to the space sector due to its promising future prospects and potential for disruptive innovation. Entrepreneurs should develop a compelling business plan and pitch to attract the interest of venture capitalists and angel investors.

3.   Crowdfunding:
In recent years, crowdfunding has emerged as an alternative and popular method for raising funds for space startups. Platforms like Kickstarter and Indiegogo allow

entrepreneurs to present their projects to a wide audience and receive contributions from individuals interested in supporting innovation in the space industry. Successful crowdfunding campaigns often require a compelling story, a clear value proposition, and an engaged community.

4. Strategic Partnerships: Collaborating with established players in the space industry through strategic partnerships can provide startups with access to financial resources, expertise, and market reach. By leveraging the strengths of both parties, startups can accelerate their growth and secure the necessary funding to bring their satellite solutions to market. Entrepreneurs should actively seek out potential partners and build mutually beneficial relationships.

5. Incubators and Accelerators: Incubator and accelerator programs specifically tailored for space startups can offer a combination of funding, mentorship, and networking opportunities. These programs provide entrepreneurs with a supportive ecosystem to refine their business models, connect with industry experts, and gain exposure to potential investors. Entrepreneurs should research and apply to reputable space-focused incubators and accelerators to enhance their chances of success.

Conclusion:
Securing funding is a critical step for space startups to transform their innovative ideas into reality. By exploring and leveraging the various funding options available, entrepreneurs can ensure the financial sustainability of their ventures and contribute to the growth and development of the space industry. With determination, strategic planning, and a solid business proposition, entrepreneurs can successfully navigate the funding landscape and propel their satellite solutions towards success.

Legal and regulatory considerations for satellite companies

As entrepreneurs in the space industry, it is crucial to be aware of and adhere to the various legal and regulatory considerations that govern satellite companies. Navigating the legal landscape is essential for ensuring compliance, protecting intellectual property, and fostering a conducive environment for innovation and growth. This subchapter will provide an overview of the key legal and regulatory considerations for satellite companies.

One of the primary considerations for satellite companies is obtaining the necessary licenses and permits. Depending on the jurisdiction, there may be specific licensing requirements for launching, operating, and providing satellite services. Entrepreneurs must engage with regulatory bodies such as the Federal Communications Commission (FCC) in the United States or the International Telecommunication Union (ITU) on an international level to secure the appropriate authorizations. Compliance with these regulations is essential to avoid penalties and ensure the smooth operation of satellite services.

Intellectual property protection is another critical aspect for satellite companies. Entrepreneurs must safeguard their innovations, technologies, and data through patents, copyrights, and trade secrets. Given the competitive nature of the space industry, protecting intellectual property is crucial to maintain a competitive edge and attract investment.

Furthermore, entrepreneurs in the satellite sector need to be aware of privacy and data protection laws. With the increasing reliance on satellite technology for communication and data transmission, ensuring the privacy and security of customer data is paramount.

Compliance with laws such as the General Data Protection Regulation (GDPR) in the European Union is essential to maintain consumer trust and avoid legal consequences.

Space debris mitigation is another vital consideration for satellite companies. As more satellites are launched into orbit, the risk of collisions and the creation of space debris increases. Entrepreneurs must adhere to guidelines and regulations related to satellite end-of-life disposal and actively contribute to the sustainability of space operations.

Finally, entrepreneurs in the satellite industry should stay informed about evolving legal frameworks and policy changes. The space industry is dynamic, and regulations are continually evolving to address emerging challenges and opportunities. By keeping abreast of these changes, entrepreneurs can adapt their strategies and ensure compliance with the most up-to-date legal requirements.

In summary, legal and regulatory considerations play a crucial role in the success of satellite companies. Entrepreneurs in the space industry must navigate licensing requirements, protect their intellectual property, adhere to privacy and data protection laws, contribute to space debris mitigation efforts, and stay informed about evolving legal frameworks. By understanding and complying with these considerations, entrepreneurs can harness the business potential of the space industry while operating within a legally sound and responsible framework.

Chapter 5: Building and Launching Satellites

Satellite design and development

In today's technological era, where space exploration and communication have become vital aspects of our lives, entrepreneurs have a unique opportunity to capitalize on the growing potential of the space industry. One of the key components of this industry is satellite design and development. This subchapter will delve into the intricacies of designing and building satellites, providing entrepreneurs in the space niche with a comprehensive understanding of this fascinating field.

Satellite design involves a multidisciplinary approach, combining engineering, physics, and computer science. Entrepreneurs looking to venture into this domain must possess a strong technical background or collaborate with experts who can guide them through the intricate process. Understanding the fundamentals of satellite design is essential to ensure the success of any space-related business venture.

The development phase of a satellite involves a series of critical steps. It begins with defining the mission objectives and requirements, followed by the design and selection of the necessary subsystems. These subsystems include communication systems, power systems, attitude control, thermal management, and payload integration. Entrepreneurs must carefully consider each subsystem to ensure optimal performance and reliability.

Furthermore, the manufacturing process of a satellite requires entrepreneurs to work closely with engineers and technicians. The selection of materials and components must be done meticulously to withstand the harsh conditions of space and ensure longevity. Assembling and testing the satellite is a crucial phase, as any flaws or malfunctions can be catastrophic and result in mission failure. Therefore, entrepreneurs must collaborate with experienced professionals to ensure the quality and reliability of the final product.

Moreover, entrepreneurs must keep abreast of the latest technological advancements in satellite design and development. Emerging technologies, such as miniaturization, 3D printing, and advanced propulsion systems, are revolutionizing the industry, offering new possibilities for entrepreneurs to explore. Staying informed and embracing these innovations will enable entrepreneurs to create cutting-edge satellite solutions that meet the evolving demands of the space industry.

In conclusion, satellite design and development is an integral aspect of the space industry that holds immense potential for entrepreneurs. By understanding the intricacies of this field and collaborating with experts, entrepreneurs can harness the business potential in the space industry. It is essential to stay updated with the latest technological advancements and continuously strive to create innovative satellite solutions. With the right knowledge, expertise, and dedication, entrepreneurs can make a significant impact in the space niche and contribute to shaping the future of space exploration and communication.

Satellite manufacturing and assembly

Subchapter: Satellite Manufacturing and Assembly

As the space industry continues to evolve, satellite manufacturing and assembly have emerged as crucial aspects for entrepreneurs looking to tap into the vast potential of the space niche. In this subchapter, we will explore the fascinating world of satellite production, discussing its importance, key considerations, and the opportunities it presents for ambitious entrepreneurs.

Satellite manufacturing is the process of building and constructing satellites, which are essential for a wide range of applications, including telecommunication, remote sensing, weather forecasting, and navigation. The demand for satellites has skyrocketed in recent years, driven by the increasing need for global connectivity and data-driven insights. This surge in demand has opened up unprecedented opportunities for entrepreneurs to enter the satellite manufacturing industry.

One of the critical considerations in satellite manufacturing is the choice of materials and components. Satellites need to withstand the harsh conditions of space, including extreme temperatures, radiation, and vacuum. Entrepreneurs must carefully select materials and components that can endure these conditions while ensuring optimal performance and longevity. This presents an exciting opportunity for innovators to develop advanced materials and technologies specifically tailored for satellite applications.

The assembly of satellites is another crucial stage in the manufacturing process. It involves integrating various subsystems, such as power systems, communication modules, sensors, and propulsion systems, into a fully functional satellite. Achieving seamless integration and compatibility between these subsystems is essential for the satellite's overall performance and reliability. Entrepreneurs can explore opportunities in developing efficient assembly techniques and automation technologies to streamline the manufacturing process and reduce costs.

Furthermore, entrepreneurs can also consider the emerging field of satellite constellations. Instead of relying on a single satellite, constellations consist of multiple small satellites working in coordination to achieve specific objectives. This innovative approach enables improved coverage, flexibility, and redundancy. Entrepreneurs can leverage the growing demand for satellite constellations by developing cost-effective manufacturing and assembly solutions tailored to these unique requirements.

In conclusion, satellite manufacturing and assembly offer immense potential for entrepreneurs in the space industry. By leveraging their innovative ideas, entrepreneurs can contribute to the advancement of satellite technology and meet the increasing demand for satellites in various sectors. Whether it's developing advanced materials, efficient assembly techniques, or catering to the emerging trend of satellite constellations, there are numerous opportunities for entrepreneurs to harness the business potential in satellite manufacturing and assembly.

Testing and quality control of satellites

In the fast-paced and ever-evolving space industry, ensuring the reliability and performance of satellites is of utmost importance. Testing and quality control play a crucial role in the success of satellite missions, and entrepreneurs in the space niche must be well-versed in these aspects to harness the full potential of their satellite solutions. This subchapter will delve into the various testing methodologies and quality control measures employed in the satellite industry, offering valuable insights and practical guidance.

The process of testing satellites begins long before they are launched into space. Extensive ground testing is conducted to evaluate the satellite's components, systems, and overall functionality. This includes thermal vacuum testing to simulate the harsh environmental conditions of space, vibration and shock testing to ensure structural integrity, and electromagnetic compatibility testing to avoid interference with other satellites or communication systems.

Additionally, entrepreneurs must be aware of different quality control measures implemented throughout the satellite's life cycle. Quality control starts from the design phase, emphasizing the use of reliable and robust components, and continues through manufacturing, assembly, and integration. Regular inspections and rigorous quality checks are performed at each stage to identify and rectify any potential issues or defects.

Furthermore, entrepreneurs should also be familiar with the concept of reliability engineering, which involves predicting and improving the reliability of satellite systems. Reliability engineering techniques, such as failure mode and effects analysis (FMEA) and fault tree analysis (FTA), help identify potential failure points and develop strategies to mitigate them. By implementing these techniques, entrepreneurs can enhance the performance and longevity of their satellites, ensuring optimal functionality throughout their mission lifespan.

To stay at the forefront of the space industry, entrepreneurs should also be cognizant of emerging trends in satellite testing. Advancements in technologies like artificial intelligence and machine learning are revolutionizing testing processes by enabling automated analysis of large datasets, enhancing diagnostic capabilities, and reducing human error. Embracing these technological advancements can streamline testing procedures, improve accuracy, and ultimately save both time and resources.

In conclusion, entrepreneurs in the space industry must prioritize testing and quality control to ensure the success of their satellite solutions. By understanding the various testing methodologies, quality control measures, and reliability engineering techniques, entrepreneurs can optimize the performance and reliability of their satellites. Additionally, staying updated with emerging trends and technological advancements in satellite testing can give entrepreneurs a competitive edge in the ever-evolving space industry.

Launching satellites into space

The process of launching satellites into space is a critical step in the space industry. For entrepreneurs in the space sector, understanding the intricacies of satellite launches is essential to harnessing the business potential in this rapidly growing industry.

The launch of a satellite involves a series of complex procedures and careful planning. It begins with the selection of a suitable launch vehicle, such as a rocket or a space shuttle, which will carry the satellite into space. Entrepreneurs must consider various factors when choosing a launch vehicle, including payload capacity, launch site location, and cost.

Once the launch vehicle is selected, the satellite is prepared for integration. The satellite undergoes rigorous testing to ensure its reliability and functionality in the harsh conditions of space. This includes environmental tests, such as vibration and thermal vacuum tests, to simulate the launch and space environment. Entrepreneurs must invest in state-of-the-art facilities and equipment to conduct these tests and meet the industry standards.

After the satellite is fully tested and integrated with the launch vehicle, the launch window is determined. This is a crucial aspect for entrepreneurs to understand, as the launch window depends on various factors, including orbital requirements, weather conditions, and coordination with other space missions. Missing the launch window can lead to significant delays and financial losses.

During the launch itself, entrepreneurs must be prepared for potential risks and contingencies. Launch failures can occur due to technical malfunctions or unforeseen events, and entrepreneurs should have contingency plans in place to mitigate these risks. Additionally, entrepreneurs need to ensure that they have the necessary insurance coverage to protect their investment in case of a launch failure.

Once the satellite is successfully launched into space, entrepreneurs can begin to reap the benefits of their investment. Satellites play a crucial role in various industries, such as telecommunications, weather forecasting, and navigation. Entrepreneurs can leverage the capabilities of their satellites to provide services and solutions that meet the growing demands of these industries.

In conclusion, launching satellites into space is a complex process that requires careful planning, testing, and risk management. For entrepreneurs in the space industry, understanding the nuances of satellite launches is essential to harnessing the business potential in this dynamic and fast-growing sector. By investing in the right launch vehicles, conducting thorough testing, and preparing for potential risks, entrepreneurs can position themselves for success in the satellite industry and capitalize on the vast opportunities presented by space.

Chapter 6: Satellite Operations and Services

Satellite communication services

In the vast expanse of space, satellite communication services have emerged as a revolutionary technology that has transformed the way we connect and communicate. This subchapter explores the various facets of satellite communication services, focusing on the immense business potential they hold for entrepreneurs in the space industry.

Satellite communication services refer to the transmission of signals, data, and information through satellites orbiting the Earth. These services have become indispensable in today's interconnected world, enabling seamless global communication, data exchange, and internet connectivity. From television broadcasting to global navigation systems, satellite communication services have paved the way for numerous applications and businesses that rely on reliable and efficient communication.

Entrepreneurs in the space industry have a unique opportunity to harness the business potential of satellite communication services. The growing demand for connectivity, especially in remote and underserved areas, presents a lucrative market for innovative entrepreneurs to explore. By leveraging satellite technology, entrepreneurs can bridge the digital divide and bring internet connectivity to regions that were previously unreachable.

One significant niche within the space industry that can benefit from satellite communication services is the space sector itself. Satellite communications play a critical role in enabling space missions, facilitating data transfer between ground control stations and spacecraft, and ensuring uninterrupted communication during space exploration. Entrepreneurs can capitalize on this niche by providing specialized satellite communication services tailored to the unique needs of space agencies, satellite manufacturers, and space research institutions.

Furthermore, the emergence of the Internet of Things (IoT) has opened up new possibilities for entrepreneurs in the space industry. Satellite communication services are essential for connecting and managing IoT devices in remote and challenging environments. Entrepreneurs can develop innovative solutions that integrate satellite communication with IoT technologies, enabling real-time monitoring, asset tracking, and data collection in fields such as agriculture, transportation, and environmental monitoring.

In conclusion, satellite communication services offer vast business potential for entrepreneurs in the space industry. Whether it is providing connectivity to underserved regions, supporting space missions, or enabling IoT applications, satellite communication services have become a cornerstone of modern communication. By embracing this technology and exploring its various applications, entrepreneurs can carve out a niche in the space industry while contributing to the advancement of global connectivity and communication.

Earth observation and remote sensing applications

Earth observation and remote sensing applications have revolutionized the way we understand and interact with our planet. In the space industry, these technologies have opened up a world of opportunities for entrepreneurs looking to harness the business potential offered by satellite solutions.

Earth observation refers to the process of collecting data and information about the Earth's surface, atmosphere, and other physical properties using satellites in space. Remote sensing, on the other hand, involves the use of sensors and instruments to gather data from a distance, without direct contact with the object or area being observed. Together, these technologies have enabled us to monitor and understand our planet like never before.

One of the key applications of earth observation and remote sensing is in environmental monitoring. Satellites equipped with specialized sensors can track changes in land use, deforestation, pollution levels, and even monitor the health of ecosystems. This information is invaluable for entrepreneurs in the space industry who are developing solutions to address environmental challenges and create sustainable businesses.

Another important application is in the field of agriculture. By using satellite imagery, entrepreneurs can monitor crop health, predict yield, and optimize irrigation and fertilization practices. This data can help farmers increase productivity, reduce costs, and improve resource management. Entrepreneurs can also develop innovative solutions for precision farming, leveraging the power of earth observation and remote sensing to create efficient and sustainable agricultural practices.

The potential of earth observation and remote sensing extends beyond Earth itself. Entrepreneurs in the space industry can leverage these technologies to explore and understand other celestial bodies, such as the Moon, Mars, and beyond. By collecting data about the composition, topography, and atmospheric conditions of these celestial bodies, entrepreneurs can develop new insights, technologies, and businesses in space exploration and colonization.

In conclusion, earth observation and remote sensing applications offer tremendous business potential for entrepreneurs in the space industry. From environmental monitoring to agriculture and space exploration, these technologies provide a wealth of data and information that can be transformed into innovative solutions and sustainable businesses. As entrepreneurs, it is crucial to recognize and harness the power of satellite solutions to create a positive impact on Earth and beyond.

Navigation and positioning services

In this digital age of advanced technology, navigation and positioning services have become indispensable for businesses operating in the space industry. Satellites have revolutionized the way entrepreneurs navigate and position their assets, providing a wide array of benefits that contribute to the growth and success of their ventures.

Satellite-based navigation systems, such as the Global Positioning System (GPS), have transformed the way entrepreneurs operate in the space industry. These systems offer precise and accurate positioning information, enabling entrepreneurs to track the location of their assets with unmatched precision. Whether it's monitoring the position of satellites, spacecraft, or even space stations, entrepreneurs can rely on satellite navigation services to ensure their assets are precisely located at all times.

Furthermore, navigation and positioning services are not limited to tracking the location of assets alone. Satellites also provide entrepreneurs with vital information on the movement and trajectory of celestial bodies. By leveraging this knowledge, entrepreneurs can plan and execute complex space missions, optimize satellite deployments, and even enhance communication with spacecraft in real-time. This level of accuracy and control has paved the way for unprecedented advancements in space exploration and research.

Moreover, satellite navigation services are not only limited to outer space. Earth-based businesses in the space industry can also benefit greatly from these services. Entrepreneurs operating in the field of satellite communications, for example, heavily rely on navigation systems to ensure their ground-based stations are optimally positioned for maximum signal strength and coverage. This ensures seamless communication between satellites and ground stations, enabling entrepreneurs to provide uninterrupted services to their clients.

In addition to navigation services, positioning services offered by satellites are equally crucial for entrepreneurs in the space industry. Satellites equipped with advanced positioning sensors provide entrepreneurs with accurate data on the orientation and alignment of their assets. This information is vital for precise maneuvering, docking, and alignment of spacecraft, simplifying complex operations and reducing the risk of accidents or failures.

In conclusion, navigation and positioning services offered by satellites have revolutionized the way entrepreneurs operate in the space industry. The accurate positioning information provided by satellite navigation systems enables entrepreneurs to track the location of their assets with unmatched precision. Furthermore, satellite-based positioning services offer crucial data on the movement and trajectory of celestial bodies, allowing entrepreneurs to plan and execute space missions with unparalleled accuracy. Whether it's optimizing satellite deployments, enhancing communication, or ensuring precise maneuvering of spacecraft, navigation and positioning services play a pivotal role in the success of entrepreneurs in the space industry. By harnessing the power of satellite solutions, entrepreneurs can unlock new business potentials and explore uncharted territories in the vast expanse of space.

Space tourism and entertainment

Space tourism and entertainment have emerged as exciting opportunities in the space industry, captivating the imaginations of entrepreneurs and space enthusiasts alike. This subchapter explores the potential of this niche sector, showcasing the business potential that lies within the realm of space tourism and entertainment.

In recent years, the concept of space tourism has transformed from science fiction to reality. With the likes of SpaceX and Virgin Galactic leading the way, the possibility of ordinary individuals venturing beyond Earth's atmosphere is becoming increasingly feasible. This presents a significant opportunity for entrepreneurs to enter the space tourism market, offering unique experiences and pioneering advancements in the field.

One key aspect of space tourism is the entertainment factor. Imagine a world where individuals can watch live concerts, sporting events, or even participate in virtual reality experiences, all from the vantage point of space. Entrepreneurs can tap into this market by developing innovative entertainment platforms that provide captivating experiences for those who venture into space. From virtual reality simulations to immersive space-themed theme parks, the possibilities are endless.

Furthermore, space tourism can also extend to educational and scientific endeavors. Entrepreneurs can collaborate with research institutions and space agencies to offer educational programs and research opportunities for students and scientists. This not only enhances our understanding of space but also creates a sustainable revenue stream for those involved in the space tourism industry.

Additionally, entrepreneurs can explore the concept of space hotels, providing luxurious accommodations for individuals visiting space. These hotels could offer breathtaking views of our planet, zero-gravity experiences, and a range of recreational activities tailored to the unique environment of space.

However, it is crucial for entrepreneurs to consider the challenges associated with space tourism and entertainment. Safety, regulatory frameworks, and the high costs involved are some of the key hurdles that need to be addressed. Collaborating with established space industry players and leveraging technological advancements will be crucial in mitigating these challenges.

In conclusion, space tourism and entertainment present lucrative opportunities for entrepreneurs in the space industry. From offering unique entertainment experiences to developing space hotels and educational programs, this niche sector is poised for growth. By harnessing the business potential of space tourism and entertainment, entrepreneurs have the chance to shape the future of the space industry and make space more accessible and enjoyable for all.

Chapter 7: Collaborating with Space Agencies and Institutions

Partnerships with government space agencies

In the rapidly evolving space industry, entrepreneurs looking to harness the business potential of satellite solutions must understand the significant role that partnerships with government space agencies play. These partnerships provide unique opportunities for collaboration, funding, and access to invaluable resources that can propel their ventures to new heights.

Government space agencies, such as NASA in the United States or ESA in Europe, possess decades of experience and expertise in space exploration, technology development, and scientific research. By forming partnerships with these agencies, entrepreneurs gain access to a vast network of knowledge and capabilities that would otherwise be difficult to obtain. This direct collaboration allows entrepreneurs in the space industry to tap into cutting-edge research, access advanced testing facilities, and leverage the expertise of seasoned scientists and engineers.

Moreover, partnerships with government space agencies often come with substantial funding opportunities. These agencies allocate significant budgets towards research and development, and they actively seek collaborations with private entities to accelerate innovation in the space industry. Entrepreneurs can benefit from government funding programs, grants, and subsidies to support the development and launch of their satellite solutions. This financial backing can help offset the high costs associated with space exploration, satellite manufacturing, and launching missions.

Additionally, partnerships with government space agencies open doors to an extensive network of industry connections and potential customers. These agencies often have established relationships with other government entities, international organizations, and private companies operating in the space industry. Entrepreneurs can leverage these connections to form strategic alliances, secure contracts, and gain access to new markets. Collaborating with government agencies also enhances an entrepreneur's credibility and reputation within the industry, which can be invaluable for attracting investors and securing future partnerships.

To maximize the benefits of partnerships with government space agencies, entrepreneurs must approach these collaborations with a clear understanding of their goals and a well-defined strategy. While the opportunities are immense, entrepreneurs must also be prepared to navigate the complexities and regulations associated with working alongside government organizations.

In conclusion, partnerships with government space agencies offer entrepreneurs in the space industry a multitude of advantages, including access to expertise, funding, resources, and industry connections. These collaborations can catapult their satellite solutions ventures to new heights, accelerating innovation and expanding market reach. By embracing these partnerships, entrepreneurs can position themselves at the forefront of the space industry revolution and unlock the full business potential of satellite solutions.

Collaborating with research institutions and universities

In the fast-paced and ever-evolving space industry, collaboration with research institutions and universities has become an essential strategy for entrepreneurs looking to harness the business potential of satellite solutions. The synergies that arise from such partnerships can lead to groundbreaking innovations, cutting-edge technologies, and ultimately, the success of your space-related venture.

Research institutions and universities offer a wealth of resources, expertise, and facilities that can significantly benefit entrepreneurs in the space niche. These institutions are at the forefront of scientific research, with access to cutting-edge technology and a pool of talented researchers and academics. By collaborating with them, entrepreneurs can tap into this vast knowledge base and gain a competitive advantage in the market.

One of the key benefits of collaborating with research institutions and universities is the opportunity for joint research and development projects. Through these partnerships, entrepreneurs can leverage the expertise of researchers and academics to address complex technical challenges, explore new applications for satellite solutions, and push the boundaries of innovation. By working together, entrepreneurs can accelerate the development of their products or services, reduce costs, and mitigate risks.

Moreover, partnering with research institutions and universities can provide access to state-of-the-art facilities and equipment. These institutions often have specialized laboratories, testing facilities, and simulation tools that entrepreneurs may not have access to otherwise. By utilizing these resources, entrepreneurs can conduct experiments, test prototypes, and validate their ideas in a controlled environment, ensuring the quality and reliability of their satellite solutions.

Collaboration with research institutions and universities also opens up avenues for attracting top talent. Through partnerships, entrepreneurs can engage with students, researchers, and academics who are passionate about space-related topics. By offering internships, research grants, or joint academic-industry programs, entrepreneurs can attract young, innovative minds and foster a culture of creativity and collaboration within their organizations.

Furthermore, collaborating with research institutions and universities can enhance the credibility and reputation of entrepreneurs in the space industry. By associating themselves with renowned academic institutions, entrepreneurs can gain the trust of potential investors, customers, and partners. This association lends credibility to their research, development, and innovation efforts, positioning them as industry leaders and increasing their chances of securing funding and partnerships.

In conclusion, collaborating with research institutions and universities is a strategic move that can greatly benefit entrepreneurs in the space industry. By leveraging the expertise, resources, and facilities of these institutions, entrepreneurs can accelerate innovation, reduce costs, attract top talent, and enhance their credibility. These partnerships have the potential to unlock new opportunities, drive growth, and position entrepreneurs at the forefront of the rapidly evolving space industry.

Leveraging international space programs and initiatives

In recent years, the space industry has witnessed a surge in international collaboration and cooperation through various space programs and initiatives. This chapter explores the immense potential and opportunities that entrepreneurs can tap into by leveraging these global endeavors.

International space programs and initiatives provide a platform for entrepreneurs in the space industry to collaborate with governments, research institutions, and other commercial entities, fostering innovation and driving business potential. By participating in these programs, entrepreneurs gain access to cutting-edge technology, expertise, and funding, enabling them to develop groundbreaking satellite solutions.

One notable international initiative is the International Space Station (ISS). Entrepreneurs can leverage this collaborative project to conduct research and development experiments in microgravity environments. The ISS offers an ideal testbed for entrepreneurs to validate their satellite technologies, paving the way for future commercial applications. Moreover, the ISS provides an opportunity for entrepreneurs to collaborate with astronauts and space agencies, expanding their networks and opening doors to new business prospects.

Another significant international space program is the Global Navigation Satellite System (GNSS). GNSS constellations, such as the American GPS, Russian GLONASS, and European Galileo, offer entrepreneurs a reliable and accurate positioning service with global coverage. By integrating GNSS signals into their satellite solutions, entrepreneurs can develop location-based services, precision agriculture solutions, autonomous vehicle navigation systems, and much more.

Furthermore, international space programs like the Artemis program, led by NASA, present entrepreneurs with opportunities to contribute to lunar exploration and colonization efforts. Entrepreneurs can collaborate with space agencies to develop innovative technologies, including lunar rovers, habitats, and resource utilization solutions. This opens up new avenues for entrepreneurship in the emerging lunar economy.

To fully leverage international space programs and initiatives, entrepreneurs need to foster strong partnerships and collaborations with international stakeholders. Engaging with space agencies, governments, research institutions, and other commercial entities can provide entrepreneurs with access to valuable resources, expertise, and funding opportunities.

In conclusion, international space programs and initiatives offer entrepreneurs in the space industry unprecedented opportunities for collaboration, innovation, and business growth. By leveraging these global endeavors, entrepreneurs can access cutting-edge technology, gain exposure to international markets, and establish themselves as key players in the rapidly evolving space industry. The potential for entrepreneurial success in this niche is immense, and those who embrace the advantages provided by international space programs will be best positioned to harness the business potential in the space industry.

Accessing resources and expertise through collaborations

In the fast-evolving space industry, entrepreneurs are constantly seeking new ways to drive their businesses forward and harness the vast potential that lies within. One powerful strategy that can propel entrepreneurs towards success is collaboration - the act of joining forces with other organizations, experts, and resources to achieve common goals. By engaging in collaborations, entrepreneurs operating in the space industry can gain access to a wide array of resources and expertise that can significantly enhance their business prospects.

One of the primary benefits of collaboration in the space industry is the ability to access crucial resources that may otherwise be out of reach for individual entrepreneurs. The space industry demands substantial financial investments, cutting-edge technology, and specialized equipment. However, by forming strategic partnerships or alliances, entrepreneurs can pool their resources and gain access to capital, cutting-edge technologies, and state-of-the-art equipment that would have been financially unattainable otherwise. Such collaborations can help entrepreneurs overcome the initial barriers to entry and facilitate their growth in the highly competitive space industry.

Moreover, collaborations offer access to a wealth of expertise and knowledge that can prove invaluable for entrepreneurs navigating the complex space sector. The space industry is characterized by its unique challenges, including regulatory complexities, technical intricacies, and intricate supply chains. By collaborating with experienced organizations, entrepreneurs can tap into a vast network of experts who possess the necessary industry knowledge, insights, and skills. These collaborations can provide entrepreneurs with guidance, mentorship, and the opportunity to learn from those who have successfully navigated the industry's hurdles before them.

Additionally, collaborations can open doors to new markets and customers. By partnering with established players in the space industry, entrepreneurs can leverage their existing customer base, distribution networks, and market reach. Such collaborations can enhance entrepreneurs' visibility and credibility, helping them establish a stronger market presence and gain access to a wider customer base. Furthermore, by collaborating with organizations that share similar goals and values, entrepreneurs can tap into new market segments and explore innovative business models, leading to increased revenue streams and accelerated growth.

In conclusion, collaborations are a powerful tool that entrepreneurs operating in the space industry can utilize to access resources and expertise that can fuel their business success. By forming strategic partnerships, entrepreneurs can gain access to vital resources, such as capital and technology, which can significantly boost their operations. Furthermore, collaborations enable entrepreneurs to tap into the wealth of knowledge and experience possessed by industry experts, helping them navigate the complex space sector more effectively. Moreover, collaborations can provide entrepreneurs with access to new markets, customers, and revenue streams. By embracing collaborations, entrepreneurs can harness the full potential of the space industry and forge a path towards sustainable growth and prosperity.

Chapter 8: Scaling and Expanding a Satellite Company

Managing growth and scaling operations

As entrepreneurs in the space industry, one of your primary goals is to harness the immense business potential that the sector offers. However, to achieve sustainable success, it is crucial to effectively manage growth and scale your operations. In this subchapter, we will explore key strategies and considerations to help you navigate the challenges and opportunities that come with scaling your space business.

1. Establishing a Strong Foundation: Before embarking on a growth trajectory, ensure that your business has a solid foundation. This includes having a clear mission, a well-defined target market, and a scalable business model. Conduct market research to identify emerging trends and potential demand drivers in the space industry, allowing you to align your growth strategy with market opportunities.

2. Building a High-Performing Team: Scaling operations requires a talented and dedicated team. Recruit individuals who possess the necessary skills and experience, and share your vision for growth. Foster a culture of innovation, collaboration, and continuous learning within your organization, empowering your team to drive growth and adapt to evolving market dynamics.

3. Strategic Partnerships: Collaboration is key to success in the space industry. Establish strategic partnerships with other companies, academic institutions, and research organizations to leverage their expertise, access new markets, and share resources. Collaborative efforts can

expedite the development of new technologies, reduce costs, and enhance your competitive advantage.

4. Scalable Technology Infrastructure: As your business grows, invest in a scalable technology infrastructure to support increased operational demands. This includes robust data management systems, secure communication networks, and advanced analytics capabilities. Embrace emerging technologies such as artificial intelligence and cloud computing to optimize operations and improve efficiency.

5. Financial Planning and Capital Allocation: Scaling operations often require significant financial resources. Develop a comprehensive financial plan that outlines your growth targets, projected revenue streams, and funding requirements. Explore various financing options, including venture capital, government grants, and strategic partnerships, to secure the necessary capital for expansion.

6. Continuous Innovation and Adaptability: The space industry is evolving rapidly, driven by technological advancements and changing market dynamics. To stay ahead of the curve, foster a culture of continuous innovation and adaptability within your organization. Encourage experimentation, invest in research and development, and actively seek customer feedback to drive product and service improvements.

7. Monitor and Evaluate Performance: Regularly monitor and evaluate key performance indicators to track the progress of your growth initiatives. Establish metrics that align with your growth goals, such as revenue growth rate, customer acquisition cost, and market share. Use this data to identify areas for improvement, make informed decisions, and adjust your strategy accordingly.

By effectively managing growth and scaling operations, you can position your space business for long-term success in this dynamic industry. Embrace collaboration, invest in technology, and foster a culture of innovation to unlock the immense potential the space sector offers.

International expansion and market entry strategies

International expansion and market entry strategies in the space industry are crucial for entrepreneurs looking to harness business potential in this rapidly growing sector. As the space industry continues to evolve and expand, entrepreneurs need to understand the dynamics of entering international markets to ensure their success.

When considering international expansion, entrepreneurs should first conduct a thorough market analysis to identify potential target markets. This analysis should include factors such as market size, competition, regulatory environment, and consumer demand. By understanding these variables, entrepreneurs can strategically select the most suitable markets for their satellite solutions.

One of the critical decisions entrepreneurs need to make is choosing the right market entry strategy. There are various options available, including exporting, licensing, joint ventures, and direct investment. Each strategy has its advantages and challenges, and entrepreneurs must carefully evaluate them based on their business objectives and available resources. For example, exporting may be a suitable initial strategy for entrepreneurs with limited resources, while joint ventures or direct investment may be more appropriate for those seeking to establish a strong presence in international markets.

Building partnerships and alliances with local players in the target markets can significantly enhance the chances of success. Collaborating with established companies or local governments can provide entrepreneurs with valuable insights into the local market, access to distribution networks, and regulatory support. These partnerships can also help mitigate risks associated with entering unfamiliar markets.

Entrepreneurs must also consider cultural differences, language barriers, and regulatory complexities when venturing into international markets. Adapting their products and services to meet the specific needs and preferences of each market is essential for success. Additionally, entrepreneurs should invest in building a diverse and multicultural team capable of understanding and navigating the challenges associated with international expansion.

Furthermore, entrepreneurs should continuously monitor and evaluate their international expansion efforts. Regularly reviewing market performance, adjusting strategies, and seeking feedback from customers and partners can help fine-tune business operations and ensure long-term success.

In conclusion, international expansion and market entry strategies are vital considerations for entrepreneurs in the space industry. By conducting thorough market analysis, selecting the appropriate entry strategy, building partnerships, adapting to local needs, and continuously evaluating performance, entrepreneurs can position themselves for success in international markets. The opportunities in the space industry are vast, and with the right approach, entrepreneurs can harness the business potential and achieve growth on a global scale.

Mergers, acquisitions, and strategic partnerships

Mergers, acquisitions, and strategic partnerships have become increasingly prevalent in the space industry, as entrepreneurs seek to harness the immense business potential that lies within this dynamic sector. In this subchapter, we delve into the significance and benefits of such collaborations, exploring how they can propel space-focused entrepreneurs towards new heights of success.

The space industry is inherently complex and capital-intensive, requiring substantial investments in research, development, and infrastructure. Mergers and acquisitions offer entrepreneurs a unique opportunity to consolidate resources, streamline operations, and gain a competitive edge in the market. By joining forces with other companies, entrepreneurs can pool their expertise, capital, and technology, accelerating their progress and reducing the time it takes to bring innovative solutions to market.

Strategic partnerships, on the other hand, enable entrepreneurs to access new markets, expand their customer base, and tap into complementary skill sets. By collaborating with established players or industry giants, entrepreneurs can leverage the reputation and market reach of their partners to enhance their own brand visibility and credibility. Moreover, strategic partnerships often facilitate knowledge-sharing and technology transfer, enabling entrepreneurs to access cutting-edge research and development resources that may have otherwise been out of reach.

In the space industry, where innovation is key, mergers, acquisitions, and strategic partnerships also foster collaboration between different sectors. Entrepreneurs with expertise in space technology can partner with companies in sectors such as telecommunications, agriculture, or transportation, to create innovative solutions that address specific industry challenges. By combining their respective strengths, entrepreneurs can unlock new business opportunities and create disruptive products or services that revolutionize entire industries.

However, it is essential for entrepreneurs to approach mergers, acquisitions, and strategic partnerships with caution and a clear understanding of their objectives. Thorough due diligence, careful negotiation, and a well-defined integration plan are crucial to ensuring the success of such collaborations. It is also important to maintain a balance between preserving the entrepreneurial spirit and embracing the benefits of scale and synergy that partnerships bring.

In conclusion, mergers, acquisitions, and strategic partnerships are powerful tools that can propel space-focused entrepreneurs towards accelerated growth and success. By leveraging the resources, expertise, and market reach of their partners, entrepreneurs can overcome the challenges inherent in the space industry and unlock new opportunities for innovation and profitability. With careful planning and execution, these collaborative ventures have the potential to reshape the future of the space industry and revolutionize the way we harness its business potential.

Challenges and considerations for global expansion

Expanding a business globally is an exciting opportunity for entrepreneurs in the space industry. However, it comes with its fair share of challenges and considerations. As you set your sights on global expansion, it is crucial to be aware of the obstacles that may lie ahead and prepare accordingly. This subchapter explores some key challenges and considerations for entrepreneurs venturing into the global space industry.

1. Regulatory Compliance: The space industry is heavily regulated by national and international bodies. As you expand globally, you need to navigate through various regulatory frameworks, including licensing, data protection, and export controls. Understanding and adhering to these regulations is imperative to ensure smooth operations and avoid legal complications.

2. Cultural and Language Differences: Global expansion means encountering diverse cultures and languages. Effective communication is vital for building relationships and developing partnerships. It is crucial to adapt your marketing strategies, product offerings, and communication styles to suit each target market. Employing local talent and utilizing translation services can help bridge the cultural and language gaps.

3. Infrastructure and Logistics: Expanding into new markets requires establishing a robust infrastructure and logistical network. The availability of suitable office spaces, transportation, and supply chain capabilities are vital considerations. Collaborating with local partners can provide valuable insights into local infrastructure and help streamline operations.

4. Market Research and Localization: Before expanding globally, thorough market research is essential. Analyze the demand for your products or services in each target market, understand the competition, and tailor your offerings accordingly. Localization of marketing materials, websites, and customer support is critical to resonate with the local audience and gain their trust.

5. Talent Acquisition and Retention: Building a skilled workforce is crucial for success in the space industry. Global expansion requires hiring talent that understands the local market, regulations, and industry nuances. Developing attractive compensation packages, fostering a diverse and inclusive work culture, and offering growth opportunities are key to attracting and retaining top talent.

6. Financial Considerations: Expanding globally requires a significant financial investment. Consider factors such as currency exchange rates, taxation laws, and funding options available in each market. Seek advice from financial experts and explore partnerships or collaborations to mitigate financial risks.

In summary, global expansion in the space industry presents immense potential but also significant challenges. By understanding and addressing these challenges, entrepreneurs can navigate the complexities of international markets, seize opportunities, and propel their businesses to new heights.

Chapter 9: Future Outlook and Trends in the Space Industry

Emerging technologies and innovations in satellite solutions

In today's rapidly evolving technological landscape, the space industry is experiencing a revolutionary transformation. Entrepreneurs and businesses operating in the space niche are constantly seeking innovative solutions to harness the vast business potential that satellites offer. This subchapter explores the emerging technologies and innovations that are shaping the future of satellite solutions.

One of the key advancements in satellite technology is the miniaturization of satellites, commonly known as CubeSats. These small, affordable satellites offer immense opportunities for entrepreneurs to launch their own space missions and gather valuable data. CubeSats are being used for a wide range of applications, including remote sensing, Earth observation, and even communication networks. Their compact size and cost-effectiveness make them a game-changer for entrepreneurs looking to enter the space industry.

The proliferation of high-speed internet connectivity has also led to the emergence of satellite internet constellations. Companies like SpaceX, OneWeb, and Amazon are investing heavily in building mega-constellations of thousands of satellites in low Earth orbit. These constellations aim to provide global broadband internet coverage, especially in underserved areas. For entrepreneurs, this presents an unprecedented opportunity to develop innovative applications and services that can leverage the connectivity provided by these constellations.

Artificial Intelligence (AI) and machine learning are also revolutionizing satellite solutions. By analyzing vast amounts of satellite data, AI algorithms can detect patterns, monitor changes, and predict future trends. This has immense implications for various industries, including agriculture, urban planning, and disaster management. Entrepreneurs can leverage AI-powered satellite solutions to develop innovative products and services that address critical challenges faced by these industries.

Another emerging trend in satellite solutions is the integration of satellite data with other technologies such as Internet of Things (IoT) and blockchain. By combining satellite data with IoT sensors and blockchain's decentralized and transparent nature, entrepreneurs can create secure and reliable systems for asset tracking, supply chain management, and environmental monitoring. This integration opens up new opportunities for entrepreneurs to develop sustainable and efficient solutions that leverage the unique capabilities of satellites.

In conclusion, the space industry is undergoing a transformative phase, and entrepreneurs in the space niche must stay abreast of the emerging technologies and innovations in satellite solutions. CubeSats, satellite internet constellations, AI, machine learning, and the integration of satellite data with other technologies are just a few examples of the exciting developments shaping the future of satellite solutions. By harnessing these advancements, entrepreneurs can unlock the vast business potential offered by satellites and contribute to the growth and evolution of the space industry.

Space exploration and colonization prospects

As entrepreneurs, it is essential to stay ahead of the curve and identify emerging industries with untapped business potential. One such industry that holds immense promise is space exploration and colonization. The possibilities that lie beyond our planet are vast, and the entrepreneurial spirit can play a pivotal role in harnessing the business potential in the space industry.

Space exploration has captivated human imagination for centuries, but recent advancements in technology have made it more attainable than ever before. This subchapter aims to explore the various prospects and opportunities in space exploration and colonization, highlighting the potential for entrepreneurial ventures to thrive in this niche.

The space industry encompasses a wide range of activities, from satellite launches and space tourism to asteroid mining and planetary research. Each of these areas presents unique business opportunities for entrepreneurs willing to take the plunge. For instance, the growing demand for satellite communication and remote sensing services has created a thriving market for satellite solutions. Entrepreneurs can leverage their expertise to develop innovative satellite technologies, offering reliable and efficient solutions to meet the needs of various industries.

Furthermore, the potential for space tourism is rapidly emerging as a lucrative business avenue. With the rise of private space companies, the dream of space travel is becoming a reality for many. Entrepreneurs can capitalize on this trend by offering space tourism packages, designing space hotels, or developing technologies for sustainable space habitats.

Another exciting prospect lies in asteroid mining, where entrepreneurs can tap into the vast resources available in space. Asteroids contain valuable minerals and metals, including platinum, gold, and rare earth elements. Developing technologies to extract and utilize these resources can revolutionize industries on Earth, creating new avenues for entrepreneurial ventures.

Moreover, the colonization of other planets, such as Mars, presents immense potential for entrepreneurs. Establishing sustainable habitats on other celestial bodies can open up new frontiers for research, manufacturing, and habitation. Entrepreneurs can contribute by developing technologies for terraforming, creating self-sufficient ecosystems, and offering logistical support for future colonization efforts.

In conclusion, space exploration and colonization offer a plethora of prospects for entrepreneurs. From satellite solutions to space tourism, asteroid mining to planetary colonization, the space industry presents a wide range of untapped business potential. By staying informed about the latest advancements and investing in innovative technologies, entrepreneurs can position themselves at the forefront of this burgeoning industry. The future of space exploration holds tremendous opportunities, and it is up to entrepreneurs to seize them and pave the way for humanity's next great frontier.

Policy and legal developments shaping the space industry

The space industry has always been a frontier for innovation and exploration. With advancements in technology and increasing interest from entrepreneurs, the sector is experiencing a renaissance. However, the growth of the space industry is not solely determined by technological advancements. Policy and legal developments play a crucial role in shaping the landscape of this unique industry.

In recent years, governments and international organizations have been actively developing policies to support and regulate the space industry. These policies aim to foster innovation, ensure safety, and promote sustainable practices. Entrepreneurs in the space sector must stay informed about these policy and legal developments to navigate the ever-evolving landscape effectively.

One significant policy development is the establishment of a regulatory framework for commercial space activities. Governments around the world are recognizing the need to create guidelines and regulations to govern the private sector's involvement in space exploration and satellite operations. This framework ensures that entrepreneurs have clear guidelines to follow, reducing uncertainty and encouraging investment in the industry.

Another critical development is the growing focus on space debris mitigation and space traffic management. As the number of satellites and space missions increases, the risk of collisions and debris accumulation in space becomes a concern. Entrepreneurs must be aware of the regulations surrounding satellite disposal and maneuverability to mitigate the risk of collisions and ensure the long-term sustainability of space activities.

Furthermore, intellectual property rights are becoming increasingly important in the space industry. Entrepreneurs must understand the legal framework surrounding patents, copyrights, and trademarks to protect their innovations and ideas. The space industry is a highly competitive field, and securing intellectual property rights can provide a competitive advantage and attract potential investors.

Lastly, international collaboration and cooperation are crucial for the future of the space industry. Governments and organizations are working together to establish international agreements and treaties to promote peaceful exploration and utilization of space. Entrepreneurs should be aware of these agreements and understand how they may impact their operations and partnerships on a global scale.

In conclusion, policy and legal developments are shaping the space industry in significant ways. Entrepreneurs in the space sector must stay informed about these developments to navigate the industry effectively. Understanding the regulatory framework, space debris mitigation, intellectual property rights, and international collaboration will be essential for entrepreneurs to harness the business potential in the space industry. By staying informed and adapting to these developments, entrepreneurs can position themselves for success in this exciting and rapidly evolving sector.

Predictions and opportunities for the future of space entrepreneurship

As entrepreneurs, it is crucial to stay ahead of the curve and identify emerging opportunities that can revolutionize industries. One such industry that holds immense potential is space entrepreneurship. The space industry has witnessed remarkable advancements in recent years, with private companies like SpaceX and Blue Origin leading the charge. In this subchapter, we will explore the predictions and opportunities that lie ahead for space entrepreneurship.

1. Satellite Internet: The demand for high-speed internet connectivity is growing exponentially. The future of space entrepreneurship lies in deploying constellations of satellites to provide global internet coverage. This opens up avenues for entrepreneurs to develop innovative applications and services that rely on seamless connectivity, including telecommunication, remote sensing, and Internet of Things (IoT) solutions.

2. Asteroid Mining: The abundance of valuable resources on asteroids presents an exciting opportunity for space entrepreneurs. As technology progresses, the mining of precious metals, minerals, and water from asteroids could become a reality. Entrepreneurs can explore the potential for resource extraction and develop sustainable methods to harness these resources for Earth's benefit.

3. Space Tourism: The space tourism sector is poised to take off in the coming years. With companies like Virgin Galactic and SpaceX already gearing up for commercial spaceflights, entrepreneurs can tap into this market by offering unique experiences, luxury accommodation in space stations, or organizing space-themed events. There is

immense potential for entrepreneurs to create a thriving industry around space tourism.

4. Space Debris Management: The increasing number of satellites and spacecraft in orbit has led to a growing concern about space debris. Entrepreneurs can seize opportunities in developing technologies to actively remove space debris, monitor orbital traffic, and ensure the long-term sustainability of space activities.

5. Lunar Colonization: Establishing a sustainable human presence on the Moon is not a distant dream anymore. Governments and private companies are actively working on lunar missions, creating opportunities for space entrepreneurs to contribute to the development of infrastructure, resource utilization, and scientific research on the Moon.

6. Interplanetary Exploration: The exploration of Mars and other celestial bodies has always fascinated humans. As space agencies and private companies plan manned missions to Mars, entrepreneurs can play a vital role in developing technology, life support systems, and solutions for long-duration space travel.

In conclusion, the future of space entrepreneurship holds immense promise. From satellite internet and asteroid mining to space tourism and lunar colonization, there is a vast array of opportunities waiting to be explored. Entrepreneurs in the space industry have the chance to shape the future by leveraging technology, innovation, and sustainability. The possibilities are limitless, and those who dare to dream big and embrace the challenges of venturing beyond our planet will undoubtedly make groundbreaking contributions to space entrepreneurship.

Chapter 10: Conclusion

Recap of key concepts and insights

In this subchapter, we will provide a comprehensive recap of the key concepts and insights discussed throughout "Satellite Solutions: Harnessing Business Potential in the Space Industry." Aimed at entrepreneurs in the niche of space, this summary will serve as a valuable reference point for those looking to navigate the complexities of the rapidly evolving space industry.

1. The Evolving Space Industry: We began by exploring the transformative changes in the space industry, highlighting the shift from government-dominated activities to increased commercial participation. This transition has opened up vast opportunities for entrepreneurs to leverage satellite solutions.

2. Satellite Technology and Applications: We delved into the various satellite technologies and applications that entrepreneurs can harness. From communication and broadcasting to remote sensing and navigation, satellites offer a multitude of possibilities for innovative business ventures. Understanding the different types of satellites and their capabilities is crucial in identifying potential markets and opportunities.

3. Market Analysis and Competitive Landscape: We emphasized the importance of conducting thorough market analysis and understanding the competitive landscape. Entrepreneurs need to identify gaps, assess market demand, and evaluate potential competitors to develop a sustainable business model and gain a competitive edge.

4. Funding and Investment Strategies: Securing funding is a critical aspect of any entrepreneurial

venture. We discussed various funding options, including government grants, venture capital, and partnerships. Furthermore, we provided insights into crafting compelling investment strategies to attract potential investors and secure the necessary resources for growth.

5. Regulatory Considerations: Navigating the space industry requires a deep understanding of the regulatory environment. We highlighted the key regulatory bodies and policies that entrepreneurs must adhere to, such as licensing requirements, spectrum allocation, and international treaties. Compliance with these regulations is crucial for long-term success in the space industry.

6. Collaboration and Partnerships: We emphasized the power of collaboration and partnerships in the space industry. Entrepreneurs can leverage alliances with established players, universities, research institutions, and other startups to gain access to expertise, resources, and market reach. Building a strong network and fostering mutually beneficial relationships can accelerate business growth.

As entrepreneurs in the space industry, it is essential to remain adaptable, innovative, and forward-thinking. By keeping these key concepts and insights in mind, you are well-equipped to harness the immense business potential that the space industry offers. Stay informed, stay connected, and seize the opportunities that lie beyond the Earth's atmosphere.

Final thoughts and encouragement for aspiring space entrepreneurs

Congratulations! If you are reading this subchapter, it means that you have embarked on an incredible journey towards becoming a space entrepreneur. The world needs more visionaries like you who are willing to push the boundaries of what is possible and harness the business potential in the space industry. As you navigate this challenging and exciting path, here are some final thoughts and words of encouragement to keep you motivated and inspired.

First and foremost, always remember that failure is not the end; it is merely a stepping stone towards success. Many of the most successful space entrepreneurs faced numerous setbacks and failures before achieving their goals. Embrace these challenges as valuable learning experiences and use them to fuel your determination and drive. Remember, it is through perseverance and resilience that great achievements are made.

In the fast-paced and ever-evolving space industry, it is crucial to stay updated and informed. Continuously educate yourself about the latest advancements, technologies, and trends shaping the space sector. Attend conferences, join industry associations, and network with like-minded individuals. Collaboration and knowledge-sharing are crucial for success in this field.

Furthermore, surround yourself with a supportive network of mentors, advisors, and fellow entrepreneurs. Seek guidance from those who have already walked the path you are embarking on. Their insights, experiences, and wisdom can prove invaluable as you navigate the complexities of the space industry.

Remember that innovation and creativity are at the core of success in the space sector. Embrace your entrepreneurial spirit and think outside the box. Seek innovative solutions to the challenges you encounter, and never be afraid to take calculated risks. Break free from conventional thinking and explore new possibilities. By doing so, you can carve out your unique niche in the space industry.

Lastly, always keep your purpose and mission in mind. The space industry offers immense opportunities to contribute to the betterment of humanity. Whether it is through advancing scientific research, improving communication systems, or addressing environmental challenges, your work as a space entrepreneur can have a profound impact on the world. Let this purpose drive you forward, even in the face of adversity.

In conclusion, aspiring space entrepreneurs, you are embarking on an extraordinary journey. Embrace failure as a stepping stone, stay informed, build a supportive network, foster innovation, and always remember the purpose behind your work. The space industry holds immense potential, and with your passion and dedication, you can harness this potential and make a lasting impact. Dream big, aim high, and never stop reaching for the stars. Good luck!

Resources and references for further exploration in the space industry

As entrepreneurs with an interest in the space industry, it is essential to stay up to date with the latest advancements, trends, and opportunities in this rapidly evolving sector. To help you navigate the vast ocean of information, we have compiled a list of valuable resources and references that will aid in your further exploration of the space industry.

1. National Aeronautics and Space Administration (NASA): The official website of NASA is a treasure trove of information, research papers, and reports related to space exploration, technology, and business opportunities. It provides insights into ongoing missions, upcoming projects, and collaborations, making it an invaluable resource for entrepreneurs in the space industry.

2. Space News: Space News is a leading publication covering the latest news, developments, and analysis across the global space industry. Their website and print magazine provide comprehensive coverage of satellite launches, industry trends, regulatory updates, and interviews with key industry leaders. Subscribing to this publication will help you stay informed about the most recent happenings in the space sector.

3. International Astronautical Federation (IAF): The IAF is an international organization that brings together industry professionals, scientists, and entrepreneurs from around the world. Their website offers access to research papers, conference presentations, and reports that cover a wide range of topics related to space exploration, technology, and policy-making.

4. Space Entrepreneurship: This book by leading space entrepreneur Robert C. Jacobson provides insights into the challenges and opportunities faced by entrepreneurs in the

space industry. It delves into the process of starting and scaling a space-focused business, offering practical advice and case studies to inspire and guide aspiring entrepreneurs.

5. Space Foundation: The Space Foundation is a non-profit organization dedicated to promoting space awareness and education. Their website features a wealth of resources, including reports, articles, and white papers on various aspects of the space industry. Additionally, they organize the annual Space Symposium, which brings together industry leaders and entrepreneurs for networking and knowledge sharing.

6. Space Angels: Space Angels is an early-stage investment firm focused exclusively on the space industry. Their website offers access to market reports, investor insights, and research papers that provide valuable information on emerging trends, investment opportunities, and the overall state of the space economy.

By leveraging these resources and references, you will be able to dive deeper into the space industry, gaining a better understanding of its potential, challenges, and avenues for entrepreneurial success. Remember, the space industry is a dynamic and rapidly evolving field, and staying informed is crucial for entrepreneurs looking to harness its business potential.